D0397516

Depression

Faye Zucker

Franklin Watts
A Division of Scholastic Inc.
New York • Toronto • London • Auckland • Sydney
Mexico City • New Delhi • Hong Kong
Danbury, Connecticut

Dedication

This book is dedicated to Joel Mark Tropper (1943-1990)

Cover illustration by Peter Cho
Cover and Interior Design by Kathleen Santini
Illustrations by Pat Rasch

Library of Congress Cataloging-in-Publication Data

Zucker, Faye.
Depression / Faye Zucker.
p. cm. — (Life balance)
Contents: The many forms of depression—The signs and symptoms of depression—Treatment for depression—Suicide: the most serious outcome of depression.
Includes bibliographical references and index.
ISBN 0-531-12259-X (lib. bdg.) 0-531-15578-1 (pbk.)
1. Depression, Mental—Juvenile literature. [1. Depression, Mental.] I. Title. II. Series.
RC537.Z83 2003
616.85'27—dc21
2003000118

Printed in the United States of America.
1 2 3 4 5 6 7 8 9 10 R 12 11 10 09 08 07 06 05 04 03

Table of Contents

One

The Many Forms of Depression

Things were bad now and would get worse later. They would. I had not heard the word *depression* yet, and would not for some time . . . , but I felt something very wrong was going on. In fact, I felt that *I* was wrong—my hair was wrong, my face was wrong, my personality was wrong—my God, my choice of flavors at the Häagen-Dazs shop after school was wrong! . . . I was one big mistake.

—Elizabeth Wurtzel, *Prozac Nation: Young and Depressed in America.* New York: Riverhead Books, 1995, p. 46.

At the age of eleven, Elizabeth Wurtzel began to understand that her dark moods were not just ordinary blues. She was experiencing the grays and blacks of depression, a disorder that can make every day seem cloudy and dreary, as if the sun never shines and as if all the feelings in the world involve sadness, helplessness, hopelessness, guilt, and discouragement.

Everyone feels blue sometimes. The blues are a normal part of everyday life. People who feel blue may be sad or grumpy or restless, but sooner or later, their blues go away, perhaps after a nap or a treat or time spent having fun with friends. Depression is a medical condition that occurs when the blues do not go away. Like Elizabeth Wurtzel, people with depression experience ordinary blues that turn gray or black and then stay that way for a long time. In the most serious cases of depression, people may feel so sad that they want to die.

Friends and family often cannot tell the difference between ordinary sadness and real depression. They may ignore the signs of real depression and pressure the depressed person to cheer up, stop moping, or snap out of it. Sometimes depression does clear up all by itself. But most of the time, just as with strep throat or a broken bone, a person with depression cannot cheer up or get better without treatment from a doctor.

Who Gets Depression?

The U.S. National Institute of Mental Health (NIMH) estimates that 18.8 million Americans have an episode of depression each year. The National Depressive and Manic-Depressive Association (NDMDA) offers statistics by age groups for people with depression in the United States:

- *1 in every 33 children*
- *1 in every 8 teens*
- *1 in every 7 adult men*
- *1 in every 4 adult women*
- *1 in every 10 new mothers following childbirth*
- *1 in every 6 elders over the age of 65*

The Biochemistry of Depression

Doctors and researchers have studied depression for a long time, focusing on how depression affects the mind, moods, and feelings. As medical research progressed, doctors made many new discoveries about the complex ways in which depression affects not just the mind, but many different parts of the body.

Today, doctors believe that depression is linked to hormones and neurotransmitters. These are chemicals inside the body that transfer information and instructions from the brain to the body about energy, growth, sleep, digestion, hunger, happiness, self-esteem, and everything else. Hormones are the chemical messengers that carry information and instructions to organs, such as the thyroid, the pancreas, and the liver. Neurotransmitters are the chemical messengers that specialize in carrying information to the brain and the nervous system.

When Neurotransmitters Work Correctly

The neurotransmitters that carry messages from the brain about happiness, self-esteem, well-being, and other

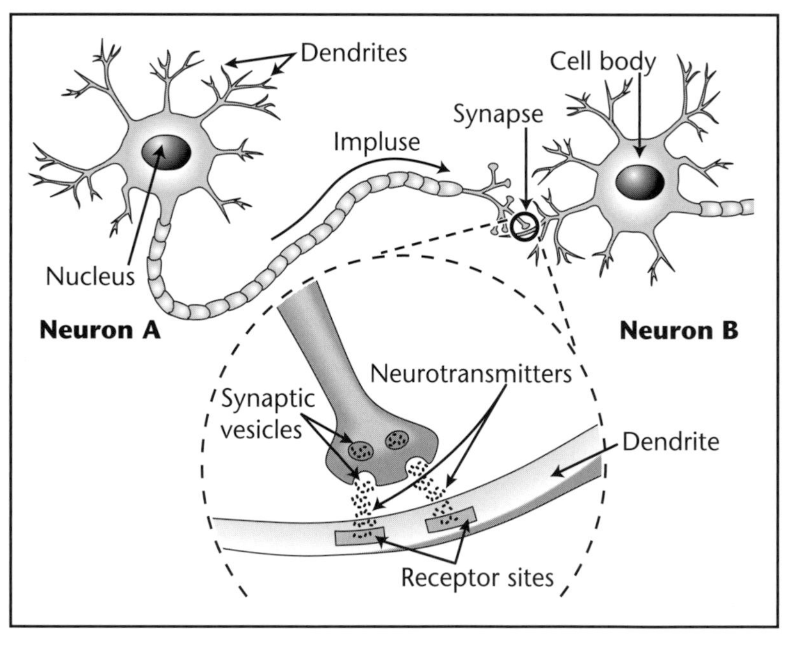

Neurotransmitters are chemical messengers that travel from one neuron (nerve cell) to the next across intercellular spaces called synapses.

moods and feelings are called norepinephrine, dopamine, and serotonin. These neurotransmitters travel from neuron (nerve cell) to neuron throughout the body's nervous system, moving from the transmitting end of one neuron to the receiving end of the next by swimming across an intercellular space called a synapse.

This is a complex process. Each neurotransmitter has its own unique chemical shape, carries its own unique chemical messages, and docks with its own unique neuroreceptors as it travels along its pathways. When neurotransmitters work correctly, we get our messages about moods and feelings clearly and right on time: "I feel happy"; "I feel safe"; "I feel sleepy"; "I feel excited"; or "I feel scared."

Serotonin and the Thanksgiving Snooze

Tryptophan is one of the essential ingredients the body needs to create serotonin, a neurotransmitter that carries messages about feelings of well-being, calmness, and relaxation. Turkey, stuffing, sweet potatoes, pecan pie, and all the other delicious foods people like to eat on Thanksgiving supply tryptophan to the body. This can cause serotonin levels in the body to increase. This could be why relaxation and napping levels increase on Thanksgiving too.

When Neurotransmitters Get Out of Balance

If something goes wrong with this process—if neurotransmitters or neuroreceptors move too quickly or too slowly, if there's a traffic jam in the synapses, or if there's too much of one neurotransmitter and not enough of another—a neurotransmitter imbalance may result. That imbalance can scramble messages about moods and feelings, which may cause depression.

Researchers do not yet understand what causes the neurotransmitter imbalances that lead to depression, but they do know that these imbalances affect the brain and the body in many different ways. Neurotransmitter imbalances may result in too little or too much energy, too little or too much sleep, too little or too much appetite, too little or too much happiness, or too little or too much self-esteem.

Many people experience serious depression only once in a lifetime. Others experience dysthymia, which makes them seem a little sad and a little blue all the time. Still others experience serious depression as a chronic (lifelong) disorder with remissions and recurrences. For months or years, people with chronic depression may feel just fine (remission), but when depression returns (recurrence), they will need treatment to keep from feeling tired, sad, and hopeless. Some forms of depression seem to run in families, which means they are linked to genetics in the same way that skin color, hair color, and size are linked to that of your parents.

The most effective treatments for depression are those that help people understand, talk about, and cope with the many ways in which neurotransmitter balances and imbalances affect their feelings and behaviors. Called psychotherapy or talk therapy (see Chapter 3), these kinds of treatment can help individuals or families adjust to depression. Sometimes, treatment for depression may include prescription medication to help the body get its neurotransmitter system back in balance.

The Different Forms of Depression

Psychiatrists are doctors who diagnose and treat mental illnesses, including depression. Many psychiatrists have special training to work with children and adolescents. Pediatricians and primary care physicians also can diagnose and treat depression, or they can help patients and families find the right psychiatrist to work with.

To determine the correct treatment, psychiatrists need to identify the form of depression that is affecting each patient. They also need to figure out whether depression is the main illness that needs treatment, or whether depression is a side effect of another medical condition that needs separate and additional treatment.

The Genetics of Depression

Some forms of depression are linked to genetics and inheritance. People with a parent, grandparent, brother, or sister who suffers from depression are more likely to have depression themselves, with the greater risk sometimes estimated at 25 percent or more than for people without a close relative with depression.

The genetic link is seen most clearly when researchers study identical twins. Identical twins have the same DNA, which is the chemical code inside every cell of the body that determines which characteristics we inherit from our parents. Researchers have found that if one identical twin has depression, the risk that the other twin also will have depression increases from 25 percent to 60–75 percent, even if the twins do not live together. But the risk is not 100 percent, which means that depression is not linked to a single gene or DNA sequence in a simple way.

So how many genes are, in fact, linked to depression? Scientists don't know yet. Current estimates are that each person has thirty thousand or more genes containing his or her DNA. The genes are organized into forty-six larger strands called chromosomes—twenty-three inherited from one's mother and twenty-three from one's father.

The mapping of all the chromosomes and the identification of their thousands of genes is the work of a massive effort known as the Human Genome Project, which has been underway since 1990. Universities and other organizations from around the world, including the United States, France, Germany, Japan, China, and the United Kingdom, are all working together on this important project, which will offer more information about the causes and treatment of depression. To learn more about the Human Genome Project, visit the Web site of the National Human Genome Research Institute (NHGRI), *www.nhgri.nih.gov*.

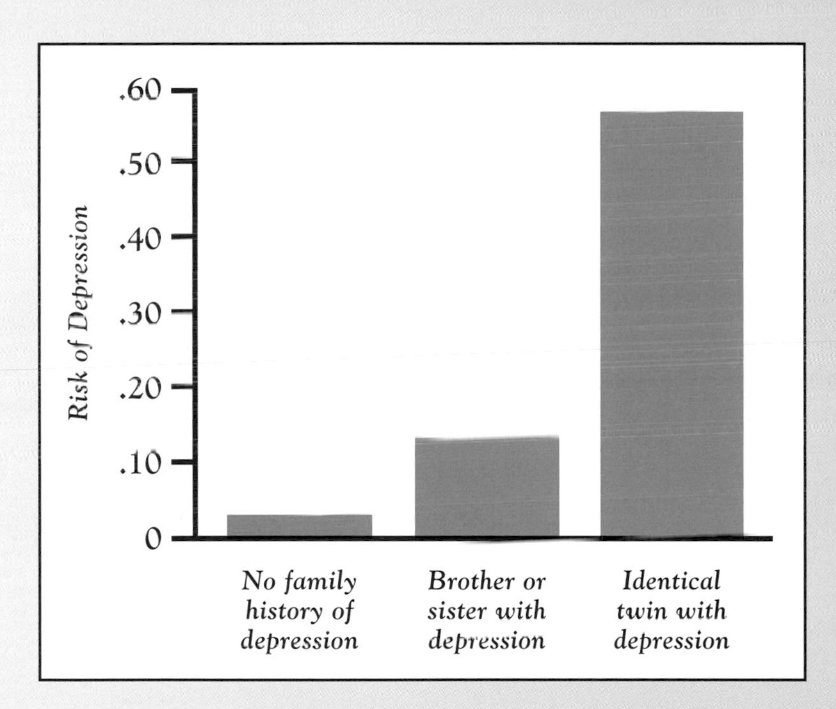

People with a parent, brother, or sister who has depression are at greater risk for depression than those without a family history of depression. The risk is greatest for identical twins.

There are questionnaires that can help people begin to determine whether they may have depression, but only a doctor can make an accurate, or correct, diagnosis. An accurate diagnosis requires a physical exam and a discussion of the person's medical history and symptoms. The doctor may use a written test or a computer questionnaire to help identify the symptoms that are unique to each person's experience with depression. Identifying the precise form of depression is essential to choosing the best treatment.

Arriving at a diagnosis may be difficult because there are many forms of depression. Each form has different signs, symptoms, durations, and treatments. Following are some of the different kinds of depression that doctors can identify and treat.

Screening for Depression

Screening for Mental Health, Inc. (www.mentalhealth-screening.org) is an information center that helps people understand mental health symptoms and find the right kinds of treatment. It offers screening programs for depression, alcoholism, eating disorders, anxiety disorders, and a high school SOS Suicide Prevention Program. This project grew out of National Depression Screening Day (NDSD), which began as an annual event in 1991 and continues to this day.

Major Depression

This is the most serious form of depression. People with major depression become so down, listless, sad, and hopeless that they cannot concentrate on the normal activities of daily living.

People with major depression do not have the energy to see their friends or do their schoolwork. They may lose interest in games, sports, and other activities that used to bring them pleasure. People with major depression may not know that their dark feelings are a medical condition. Instead, they may believe that life is hopeless and that their dark moods are their own fault. Like Elizabeth Wurtzel, they may believe that their whole existence is "one big mistake."

Major depression is a very serious medical condition that requires medical treatment. Without treatment, people with major depression may feel so down and hopeless that they fail at school or lose control of their lives. In extreme cases, people with major depression may feel so bad that they want to die. They may try to harm themselves or others.

Dysthymia

Dysthymia causes a milder form of sadness and emptiness than major depression. People with dysthymia may not stop their involvement in daily activities the way people

Myths and Facts About Depression

The U.S. National Institute of Mental Health has identified myths, or false ideas, that many people believe about depression. These are some of the most common myths:

Myth:	Fact:
Teens don't suffer from "real" depression. It's normal for them to be moody.	Depression can affect people of any age, race, ethnicity, or economic group.
Teens who say they are depressed are just weak and need to pull themselves together. There is nothing anyone else can do to help.	Depression is not a weakness. It is a serious health disorder. Both young people and adults who are depressed need professional treatment.

Myth:	Fact:
Talking about depression only makes it worse.	Talking through feelings may help a friend recognize the need for professional help. With support from a friend, a teen with depression may be able to talk to his or her parents or another trusted adult, such as a teacher or coach, about getting treatment.
Telling an adult that a friend might be depressed is betraying a trust. If someone wants help, he or she will get it.	Depression is a drain on energy and self-esteem. It interferes with a person's ability or wish to get help. Many parents may not understand the seriousness of depression or of thoughts about death or suicide. In fact, many teens and parents may not know that there is help available. It is an act of true friendship to contact a parent, a school guidance counselor, a coach, a favorite teacher, or another trusted adult when a friend talks about depression or shows signs of having depression.

with major depression do, but dysthymia does cause a form of sadness that seems to go on and on for years.

Depressed Mood During an Adjustment to Change

This is a form of depression that sometimes occurs during an adjustment to change or in reaction to a serious life event. Change and serious life events happen to people all the time, and everyone has their own definition of what makes an event serious and life changing. Ordinarily, people mostly adjust to change with patience, humor, faith, and support from friends and family. But sometimes people seem to shut down during the adjustment period, as if they have been pushed too far or too fast. That shutdown is a form of depression, and it may be a kind of time-out that allows people to adjust to the changes in their lives.

Reactive depression may follow a move to a new home or school; dealing with a divorce; not achieving an important goal, like joining a soccer team or winning a championship; or learning that one has a serious illness. Grief over the death of a family member, friend, or pet also can cause this kind of depression.

After a period of adjustment, reactive depression often clears up, allowing life to return to its day-to-day ups and downs. Receiving counseling or therapy for reactive depression can help the adjustment process.

Seasonal Affective Disorder

Seasonal affective disorder (SAD) is a form of depression that may occur when the summer season ends and the shorter days of autumn and winter begin. SAD is not just moping because summer vacation has ended and it is time to go back to school. SAD is a feeling of having no energy to wake up in the morning and get out of bed.

Scientists believe that SAD is brought on by the darker, shorter days of autumn and winter. They believe that darkness may signal the body to produce too much of the sleepy-time hormone melatonin, and that too much melatonin in the body may cause depression. When the longer, sunnier days of spring and summer arrive, SAD goes away by itself. During the winter months, doctors sometimes treat SAD with special lights, a treatment that is called phototherapy, or light therapy.

Postpartum Depression

This is a form of depression that affects fewer than one in ten new mothers after pregnancy and childbirth. Many new mothers experience the "baby blues" after giving birth, which go away on their own after a few days. Postpartum depression is a more serious case of the baby blues. A new mother with postpartum depression may be weepy or panicky, or too wakeful when her baby is sleeping. She even may have scary thoughts about harming herself or her new baby.

Scientists believe postpartum depression may be caused by rapid changes in the levels of hormones a mother produces during pregnancy and childbirth. Doctors often treat it with a skin patch that helps balance those hormones. Without treatment, postpartum depression sometimes turns into a much more serious condition called postpartum psychosis (a loss of contact with reality). In this case, mothers actually may harm themselves or their children.

Bipolar Disorder (Manic Depression)

This is a form of depression in which people go back and forth between extreme emotions—the lowest lows of major depression and the highest highs of feeling like they are on top of the world.

Originally called manic-depressive disorder, bipolar disorder creates a roller coaster of moods that goes from high (mania) to low (depression) and back again over a period of weeks, months, or years. During a depressive low, a person with bipolar disorder will be sad, hopeless, and without energy. During a manic high, those feelings change to the opposite extreme. The person who used to be depressed is suddenly wildly happy and can seem too confident, too impatient, or too reckless. Once slow and tired, he or she becomes too energetic, too wakeful, and too ready to start a million new projects all at once.

People with bipolar disorder often do not want to see a doctor for treatment during their manic highs. Their highest highs can make them feel superpowerful and superconfident, and they prefer the highs to the hopelessness of their depression. But the highs of mania can cause serious harm to people with bipolar disorder, and to their families and friends. Finding the right treatment is very important.

Cyclothymia

This is a form of bipolar disorder in which the swings from high to low and back again happen frequently, sometimes as often as daily. The highs and lows may not be as extreme as in bipolar disorder, but the roller coaster still keeps going up and down for a very long time. Sometimes children and teens with cyclothymia seem to change their moods from high to low so quickly and so often that their parents and teachers think they have attention deficit/hyperactivity disorder (ADHD). ADHD is a disorder that interferes with focus, concentration, and steady thinking. The treatment for ADHD differs from the treatment for cyclothymia and bipolar disorder, which makes a correct diagnosis extremely important.

Two

Signs and Symptoms of Depression

That summer, I am just thirteen, everything sucks and I am stuck at camp... One day right after cleanup period, right after our beds have been inspected for hospital corners and our cubbies have been checked to make sure all the *Archie* comics are piled neatly, I sit on the porch of my bunk listening to Bruce Springsteen's first album. Paris, a girl I also go to school with, comes outside to sit with me. . . . I've known her since kindergarten, and like everyone else who's been in my life for a while, she's just kind of waiting for me to snap out of this funk so that we can have play dates and polish our nails in baby pink like we used to do when we were seven. . . .we still walk home from school together sometimes, which can't be any fun for her because all I want to talk about is the oncoming apocalypse in my brain.

—Elizabeth Wurtzel, *Prozac Nation: Young and Depressed in America.* New York: Riverhead Books, 1995, p. 60.

Depression has many signs and symptoms. Signs are outward signals that other people can see. Symptoms are what people feel on the inside.

At the age of thirteen, Elizabeth Wurtzel knew she had the symptoms of depression. She knew that she believed life was sad, hopeless, and terrible, and that things would never go right and never get better. Elizabeth also knew her family and friends, like Paris, could see the outward signs of depression that had taken over her life. They could see that she was sleeping more than usual, crying for reasons she could not explain, angry for reasons that never went away, and that she had stopped wanting to do all the things that used to be fun for her. The signs and symptoms of depression were affecting every aspect of Elizabeth's life: her feelings, thoughts, behavior, and physical body.

Twelve Signs of Depression

People with depression usually have two or more of the following signs and symptoms lasting for two or more weeks:

1. *Problems with sleep*
2. *Problems with lack of energy*
3. *Problems with appetite and body weight*
4. *Problems with headaches and stomachaches that do not go away*
5. *Problems with anger, boredom, or a loss of interest in people, activities, and pleasures*
6. *Restlessness or jitteriness*
7. *Feeling angry or sad and empty*
8. *Feeling discouraged and hopeless*
9. *Feeling worthless and guilty*
10. *Thinking jumbled thoughts without concentration or focus*
11. *Forgetting events that used to be considered important and special*
12. *Thinking or talking about death or suicide*

Changes in the Body

Depression is linked to imbalances in the body's hormones and neurotransmitters (see Chapter 1). These imbalances result in a disturbance of normal patterns of sleep, energy, appetite, and pain. Changes may include:

Trouble falling asleep or staying asleep. People with

depression may wake up in the middle of the night, every night, and not be able to fall back to sleep. Sometimes people with depression sleep too much.

Fatigue and lack of energy. People with depression may feel as if their arms and legs are too heavy to move. They may not be able to get out of bed in the morning. This may happen every morning, even if they get the right amount of sleep at night.

Too small an appetite or too large an appetite. People with depression may gain weight or lose weight even if their appetite does not become disturbed.

Headaches and stomachaches that never go away. Younger children may not be able to describe these physical changes, but the people around them may notice that these problems are affecting their everyday behavior.

Changes in Behavior

People with depression experience changes in their interests, activities, and movements. Changes may include:

Becoming bored and losing interest in people and things they used to care about and enjoy. People with depression may stop caring about hobbies, games, sports, music, dating, and spending time with friends.

Stopping everyday activities. People with depression may seem to want only to stay at home in bed, never wanting to take a shower, put on clean clothing, or go outside for events they used to enjoy. Children may stop wanting to leave home or go to school. Adults may stop wearing appropriate clothing, shopping for groceries, or going to work.

Drinking alcohol or using street drugs. People with depression may start using drugs, drinking too much alcohol, staying out all night, or taking reckless risks with bikes, skateboards, and cars. Even teens and very young children may do these things because of depression.

Changing mannerisms. People with depression may seem to move more slowly than they used to. They may seem to slump over at times when they used to stand tall, straight, and strong. They also may seem fidgety, or jittery, or restless at times when they used to seem focused and calm.

These changes in behavior often are the first signs of depression noted by family and friends. It is very important to report them to doctors during checkups.

Changes in Feelings

Depression is linked to serious changes in emotions and feelings. People with depression experience not just everyday blues, but the grays and blacks of darker moods. Changes may include:

Feelings of sadness and emptiness. People with depression do not feel the happiness and joy of everyday pleasures,

Depression in Literature

Many people are familiar with depression only through reading about characters in stories or novels. One of the most famous literary cases of depression can be found in William Shakespeare's play *Hamlet* (c. 1602). The play centers on a young prince named Hamlet in the medieval kingdom of Denmark. Hamlet experiences a family crisis when his uncle murders his father and marries his mother. By the end of the play, there is dueling, poison, revenge, and war, but throughout the play, Hamlet struggles with a feeling that he is living in a world he describes as "weary, stale, flat, and unprofitable. . . ." Hamlet's sleeplessness, restlessness, hopelessness, anger, and loss of interest in his loved ones and his friends are all signs of depression. His famous speech that starts with the words "To be or not to be" is considered a classic portrait of a person with depression so severe that he has begun to consider suicide.

Nearly four centuries later, author J. K. Rowling has created another fictional case of depression. The Harry Potter books include Moaning Myrtle, a ghost with depression who haunts the girls' bathroom on the first floor of Hogwarts School for Witchcraft and Wizardry. Myrtle has a glum face, a weepy disposition, and the knowledge that everyone at Hogwarts calls her "miserable, moaning, moping Myrtle." Myrtle almost never finds the energy to leave her gloomy bathroom. She spends most of her time by herself, weeping or sitting in the U-bend of the plumbing, thinking about death.

Also fictional, but believed by many people to be autobiographical (based on the life of the author), is Sylvia Plath's *The Bell Jar* (1963). This is a novel about a young woman named Esther who feels trapped inside a bell jar of depression as she watches life pass her by. The novel describes Esther's illness and treatment, which includes an early version of electroconvulsive therapy (ECT), as well as hospitalization following a suicide attempt. Sylvia Plath was both a poet and a novelist, and she herself committed suicide in 1963.

Many other writers who struggled with depression wrote memoirs about their illnesses and attempted to describe their darkest feelings. In *Darkness Visible* (1990), William Styron described depression as "a dark storm" and "a howling tempest." Tracy Thompson called her book about depression *The Beast: A Journey Through Depression* (1996, pbk). She wrote about how difficult it was for her to accept that depression is an illness instead of a punishment for being a bad person. Dr. Kay Redfield Jamison's book about bipolar disorder is called *An Unquiet Mind: A Memoir of Moods and Madness* (1995), and Andrew Solomon named his illness and his book about it *The Noonday Demon: An Atlas of Depression* (2001). Solomon's *Noonday Demon* won the 2001 National Book Award in the United States.

such as eating, playing, laughing, and spending time with family and friends. They may seem to be tearful or crying all the time for reasons they cannot explain and their family and friends cannot understand.

Feelings of anger. People with depression may be angry at other people for reasons they cannot explain. This anger may not go away, even if other people offer apologies or change their behavior in response to the anger.

Feelings of discouragement and hopelessness. People with depression cannot seem to remember that they used to have happy feelings and pleasures before their depression began. They worry that their feelings will continue to get worse, and they lose hope that anyone can help them feel better.

Feelings of worthlessness and guilt. People with depression sometimes believe that they deserve their feelings of sadness and hopelessness. They believe that they failed to work hard enough to achieve impossible goals, that they make more mistakes than everyone else does, and that other people see them as failures.

The feelings of depression are often the symptoms that keep people from going to the doctor for treatment. These changes in how people *feel* about themselves during depression also are closely linked to how people with depression *think* about themselves.

Changes in Thoughts

Family and friends who notice these changes in behavior may also notice that people with depression think and talk about themselves in darker ways than they did before the depression began. Changes may include:

Thoughts that seem jumbled. People with depression may not be able to concentrate. They may not be able to make decisions. They may not be able to pass tests in subjects that used to be easy for them. They may not remember important things, such as birthday parties or their favorite television programs.

Thoughts that are very negative. People with depression may say that they do not deserve to be healthy and happy. They may talk about running away from home. They may believe that medical treatment for depression will not work, or that it may work for others, but not for them. They may even believe that no one wants them to get treatment or to feel better.

Thoughts about death and suicide. Without treatment, the negative thoughts of depression may turn into thoughts about death and suicide. In the most serious cases, people with depression may believe that family and friends would not miss them if they died. They may also believe that death is the only way to end the painful feelings and thoughts of depression.

Family and friends who hear people with depression expressing jumbled or negative thoughts need to encourage them to get treatment. People who talk about death or suicide need to be taken very seriously.

Four Things You Can Do If You Think You Have Depression

1. *Take a chance that asking an adult for help can help make you feel better.*
2. *Ask your parents to take you to the doctor. If you have symptoms of depression, you are not feeling well and you need to see a doctor.*
3. *Ask your school counselor to refer you to a mental health specialist.*
4. *Tell the doctor that you think you have depression and you need help.*

Changes During the Bipolar Cycle of Depression and Mania

People with bipolar disorder experience the symptoms of depression described above, but in cycles. Sometimes, they feel the lowest lows of depression, but sooner or later their moods swing to the highest highs of mania, which can make them feel as if they are all-powerful. Following is how the cycles compare.

Depression	Mania
Spends too much time in bed sleeping	Never seems to need sleep
Has too little energy	Seems too busy, too fast, too noisy
Loses interest in normal activities	Spends too much time on too many activities
Feels sad and weepy	Feels giddy, silly, elated
Feels hopeless	Feels as if the impossible is possible
Feels powerless	Feels like the most powerful person in the world
Feels worthless	Feels like the most important person in the world

During periods of mania, people with bipolar disorder feel great or even better than great, but there is a real risk that they may harm themselves or others. That makes it very important for their families to have an action plan they can use to cope with extreme behaviors that may occur during manic highs.

Whether depressive or manic, the symptoms of depression and bipolar disorder can take over one's life completely. With the right treatment, however, people with depression can get their lives back under control.

Three

Treatment for Depression

And then something just kind of changed in me. Over the next few days I became all right, safe in my own skin. It happened just like that. One morning I woke up, and I really did want to live, really looked forward to greeting the day, imagined errands to run, phone calls to return, and it was not with a feeling of great dread, not with the sense that the first person who stepped on my toe as I walked through the square may well have driven me to suicide. It was as if the miasma of depression had lifted off me, gone smoothly about its business, in the same way that the fog in San

Francisco rises as the day wears on.

—Elizabeth Wurtzel, *Prozac Nation: Young and Depressed in America.* New York: Riverhead Books, 1995, p. 329.

Treatment for Elizabeth took more than ten years and required medication, psychotherapy (talk therapy), and even periods of hospitalization. But treatment eventually worked for her, and it can work for you, too.

Many people with depression receive treatment from their primary care physicians, but pediatricians and primary care physicians often refer patients to psychiatrists. Psychiatrists are doctors with special training in the diagnosis and treatment of depression and other mental health disorders. Diagnosing the specific form of depression affecting each patient is the first step any doctor takes before prescribing treatment.

Diagnosis

Reaching a diagnosis may require multiple doctor visits. Diagnostic steps usually include physical examinations, medical histories (allergies, prior illnesses, immunizations), a family medical history (illnesses that affected parents, grandparents, brothers, and sisters), and questionnaires.

Physical examinations help to identify the parts of the brain and the body involved in the depression. They also help identify other medical conditions that may be causing or contributing to the depression. If these conditions are treated, the depression often clears up. An imbalance in the body's thyroid gland, for example, can affect the pace of metabolism. Metabolism refers to the chemical changes that take place inside the body to create energy. A metabolism that is too fast or too slow may cause feelings that seem like depression. Medication that helps rebalance thyroid hormones can return metabolism to its correct pace, which may also take care of the depression.

Medical histories are important both for the patient and for the patient's family. When taking a medical history, the doctor will ask the patient about the feelings, thoughts, and behaviors that may be symptoms of depression. The doctor will ask whether the patient thinks about or talks about death and suicide. The doctor will ask family members about signs of depression that they may have observed. The doctor also will ask about other family members, including grandparents, who may have had depression, because researchers now know that depression has a strong link to genetics and family history.

The written questionnaires and computer tests that doctors use are called screening inventories. These questionnaires help patients find the right words to describe the complex thoughts, feelings, and behaviors that are their symptoms of depression. These questionnaires have long names, like the Children's Depression Inventory (CDI), the Beck Depression Inventory (BDI), the Hamilton Depression Scale (HDS), and the Kiddie Schedule for Affective Disorders and Schizophrenia (K-SADS). No matter how long or complicated the name of the questionnaire, the purpose is the same: to help doctors identify the precise form of depression affecting a patient. This helps the doctor to prescribe the most effective treatment or combination of treatments.

Many doctors believe that the most effective treatment for depression is a combination of prescription medication and psychotherapy, also called talk therapy. The medication helps make the symptoms of depression less severe so that the patient can talk to and work with a psychotherapist. Working with a psychotherapist can help the patient learn to understand the depression and learn effective ways to cope with it.

Psychotherapy

The psychiatrist who reaches the diagnosis of depression sometimes offers psychotherapy treatment as well, but more often, psychotherapy takes place in the office of a psychologist, social worker, or mental health counselor.

Psychotherapy may be private, with just the therapist and the patient, or it may involve the patient's family. Often, people with depression work in support groups or in therapy groups with several other patients who also have depression. Many people work out therapy schedules that mix individual sessions with therapy groups.

Psychotherapy never involves injections, shocks, pills, or anything that hurts. Psychotherapy is talk therapy. Sometimes a therapist will use toys, dolls, crayons, photographs, or sand trays to make talking easier, but the most important activity is always talking about thoughts, feelings, and behavior.

The therapist's office often has comfortable chairs, couches, and pillows on the floor to help patients feel safe and comfortable. Sometimes, the therapist's office has curtains and soundproofing so that no one in the waiting room or outside the office can see or hear what goes on. This helps to protect the patient's privacy.

In talk therapy, the psychotherapist and the patient concentrate on creating a safe and trusting relationship for working together as they develop techniques for changing the negative thoughts, feelings, and behaviors of depression. Sometimes, the therapist will give homework assignments to help the patient practice new behaviors to get through the tougher times of the depression.

Finding the Right Psychotherapist

Parents, pediatricians, and school counselors can help you find a good therapist, but only you can decide if that therapist is the right one. Here are some things to consider:

- *Understanding:* Do you believe this therapist remembers and understands what it is like to be a teen, with or without depression?

- *Honesty:* Do you believe this therapist will tell you the truth about your illness and your treatment?

- *Respect:* Do you believe this therapist will treat you respectfully, even when you need to say things that adults don't like to hear?

- *Support:* Do you believe this therapist will support the decisions you make about your illness and your treatment, even if your parents don't like your decisions?

- *Empathy:* Do you believe this therapist can like you, understand what you are going through, and care about helping you to feel better?

If you don't know the answers to these questions, ask the therapist and then listen carefully to what he or she has to say. If you feel you could come to trust this person, then you have found the therapist who is right for you.

For example, a homework assignment for a patient who has lost interest in his or her favorite activities might be to watch two movies between therapy appointments or to play two video games. Sometimes, the therapist will reward the patient for accomplishing these goals.

Psychotherapy treatment often involves going to the therapist's office once each week for ten or twelve weeks, or sometimes longer. Usually, the talk therapy continues until the patient feels the symptoms of depression have improved. Patients often feel ready to end psychotherapy treatment when symptoms improve. A good therapist will support that decision, but will also remind the patient that he or she may return to therapy if the symptoms return.

Cognitive-Behavioral Therapy

Cognitive-behavioral therapy (CBT) is one of the most effective forms of psychotherapy for depression because it focuses both on thoughts (cognition) and on behavior. CBT can help people learn new ways to think about themselves, their behavior, and their illness. For example:

- People whose depression makes them think they are worthless failures ("I never do anything right") can learn techniques to remind themselves of all the times they did things right.

- People whose depression makes them think that they must achieve impossible goals ("I must get an A+ on every assignment or I will be a complete failure") can learn techniques for changing impossible goals into realistic ones.
- People whose depression makes them think that no one cares for them ("They wouldn't even notice if I ran away") can learn to recognize the signs of caring and support that may be all around them, but are clouded from view by the depression.

Many research studies have shown that the long-term effectiveness of CBT is far greater than treatment with medication alone.

Psychiatric Medication

Because depression is linked to imbalances in the body's complex chemistry of genes, proteins, hormones, and neurotransmitters (see Chapter 1), the most effective medications for depression are the ones that target specific neurotransmitters to make sure they are working correctly. When neurotransmitters are working correctly, we can take life's ordinary ups and downs in stride. When our neurotransmitters get out of balance, ordinary events can feel like tragedies that will never end. By keeping neurotransmitters working correctly, psychiatric medications can ensure that the brain's messages get delivered promptly and correctly to the rest of the body.

Medication to treat depression (antidepressant medication) is usually prescribed by a psychiatrist. It may take several tries before the psychiatrist finds the most effective medication, and it may take two to four weeks before the medication starts to take effect in a noticeable way. Once the right medication takes effect, the patient may need to continue taking it for about a year. Patients with chronic (long-term) depression may need to continue taking medication indefinitely. Sometimes a psychiatrist will need to prescribe a combination of medications. This often happens with people who have bipolar disorder. It is important to follow the doctor's instructions about taking medication and always discuss with the doctor when and how to stop taking medication.

Sometimes psychiatric medications cause unwanted side effects, especially if they have a bad interaction with food, alcohol, or another prescription medication. Unwanted side effects may include nausea, headaches, dizziness, high blood pressure, liver problems, or muscle problems. It is important for people taking medications to be monitored by their doctors on a regular basis. The doctor can check for these side effects and adjust the medication if necessary.

Medications for depression and other medical conditions do not become available for people to use until after they have been researched, tested in a laboratory, and then studied in clinical trials that test their safety and effectiveness on real people. People who receive prescriptions for psychiatric medications must visit their doctors frequently to make sure the medications continue to work without causing any harmful side effects.

Four Ways to Ask for Help

1. *If asking to see a psychiatrist or psychotherapist is too scary, ask to see a pediatrician or your regular family doctor.*
2. *If you have trouble finding the right words to describe your sadness or your anger, take this book with you. Let the doctor know that this book talks about how you feel inside.*
3. *If you can only read this book in the library, ask the librarian to photocopy the list "Twelve Signs of Depression" (p. 25) so you can take it with you. Then show the list to your doctor.*
4. *Use the Web sites in the Further Resources list (p. 72). Find the Web site that describes your depression and take information from that Web site with you to the doctor.*

Clinical Trials

Clinical trials are experiments on real people that must take place before a new medication can be approved for use. Because clinical trials are experimental, only researchers and volunteers who have been carefully chosen are allowed to participate.

During a clinical trial, volunteer patients are divided into two or more groups. One group receives the experimental medication or treatment that is being studied. The second group receives a placebo (substitute), which may be a sugar pill, or water, or something else that is disguised to look like the experimental treatment. Then the two groups are studied over a period of time to see whether the real treatment improves symptoms without causing unwanted or dangerous side effects.

Volunteer patients and the researchers who study them follow careful rules. The researchers must explain the risks and dangers in advance to the volunteers. The volunteers or their parents must sign an informed-consent document stating that they understand that the research may not help them and it may have risks.

Both volunteers and researchers often follow a "double-blind" procedure, which means they all agree in advance to let themselves be fooled by the placebo for the purpose of research. The volunteer patients do not know whether they are receiving the real treatment or the substitute. The researchers do not know whether the volunteers whom they are studying have received the real treatment or the substitute.

These rules and procedures are always carefully followed before a new medication is approved for use. This process allows researchers to identify effective treatments, to rule out treatments that do not improve symptoms, and to make sure that treatments that may cause harm are not approved for use.

Most clinical trials involve adult volunteers. Clinical trials for children and teens are done less often to prevent experimental treatments from getting in the way of healthy growth and development.

Furry, Four-Legged Therapists

Pet therapy may be the most fun treatment for depression. Research has shown that pets and companion animals can help improve symptoms of depression linked to bereavement, cancer, and AIDS. Trained therapy animals also participate in regularly scheduled visits to hospitals and nursing homes.

Electroconvulsive Therapy (ECT)

Originally called shock therapy or electroshock therapy, electroconvulsive therapy (ECT) is sometimes prescribed for severe depression or bipolar disorder. Psychotherapy and medication are usually the most effective treatments, but sometimes patients cannot cope with the side effects of

R_X Depression

The scientists who study psychiatric medications are called psychopharmacologists. Their research focuses on how neurotransmitters work in the body and how medications can improve neurotransmitter functioning if it gets out of balance. Psychopharmacology is a very new science. Its researchers have created many new medications during recent decades. Each new generation of medications targets neurotransmitters more effectively, while causing fewer unwanted side effects.

The neurotransmitters that are usually affected by depression medications are norepinephrine, serotonin, and dopamine. Medications like fluoxetine (brand-name Prozac) or sertraline (Zoloft), for example, are called selective serotonin reuptake inhibitors (SSRIs). That means they help to keep serotonin working actively in the body to create feelings of happiness, comfort, and safety that combat feelings of depression.

There is some disagreement about the use of SSRIs, particularly for children and teens. A small number of patients using SSRIs have reported that they began to think about death and suicide. This unusual result of taking medication is very rare, but psychiatrists who prescribe SSRIs must prepare patients and their families for this possibility. Patients must be monitored carefully for as long as they remain on the medication.

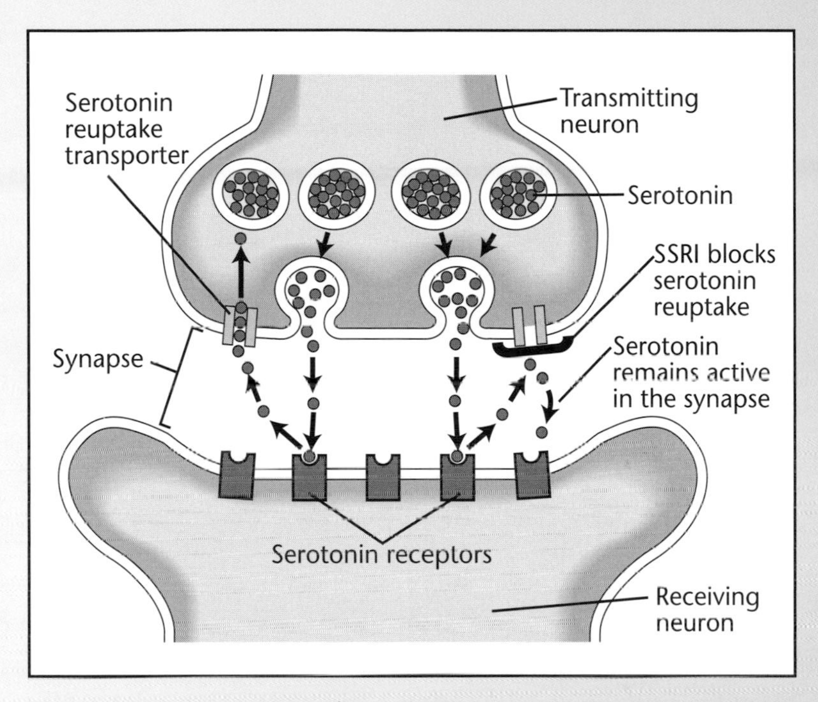

Selective serotonin reuptake inhibitors (SSRIs) keep serotonin active by blocking the cell receptors that absorb serotonin before it has finished working.

Prescription medications have two names. The *generic* name identifies the chemical makeup of the drug. The *brand* name is usually a shorter name that is given to the drug by its manufacturer. A brand name is trademarked, or protected, by the pharmaceutical companies that paid for the medication's research and development. These are some of the better known medications in use today to treat depression and bipolar disorder:

R_X Depression (*continued*)

Generic name	*Brand name*
amitriptyline	Elavil
bupropion	Wellbutrin
carbamazepine	Tegretol
citalopram	Celexa
clomipramine	Anafranil
fluoxetine	Prozac
imipramine	Tofranil
lithium	Eskalith
nefazodone	Serzone
paroxetine	Paxil
sertraline	Zoloft
tiagabine	Gabitril
tranylcypromine	Parnate
venlafaxine	Effexor

Many people believe that an herbal remedy called Saint-John's-wort (*Hypericum perforatum*) is also an effective treatment for depression. Saint-John's-wort is believed to target the same neurotransmitters as prescription medications, but researchers do not yet have proof of its effectiveness. They do know that Saint-John's-wort may cause side effects in adults taking other medications. They recommend talking to a doctor before taking Saint-John's-wort or any other over-the-counter medication. Children, teens, and women who are pregnant should avoid Saint-John's-wort entirely.

medication, cannot wait two to four weeks for medication to start working, or do not respond to medication.

In cases where medication is not effective, or if the depression is so severe that patients may be at risk of harming themselves or others, ECT may be recommended. ECT involves sending carefully controlled electrical pulses to the brain to cause a brief seizure. The seizure is like a jump start to a car battery or a reboot to a computer system. It helps the system get back on-line so the neurotransmitters can continue their work, carrying information about feelings, thoughts, and behavior. Once the neurotransmitters get back to work, the patient begins to feel improvement in the symptoms of depression and can return to psychotherapy treatment. ECT treatment also may allow people with depression more time to find the right medication.

ECT is *not* like a lightning bolt or a Frankenstein movie. ECT takes place in a hospital while the patient is in a deep sleep created by anesthesia. During ECT, the patient's heart rate, blood pressure, and breathing are carefully monitored. The patient receives muscle-relaxing medication so that the body is not injured during the seizure. The patient wakes up after ECT and usually goes home as soon as the effects of the anesthesia wear off.

Sometimes people experience memory loss, headaches, and muscle aches after ECT. Usually, those side effects go away after a day or two, and people with depression continue with their ECT treatments because the side effects are less troublesome than the severe symptoms of depression that are being treated.

ECT treatment is controversial, however. Some doctors believe that it is not a safe treatment, and many states do not permit doctors to prescribe ECT for anyone younger than age eighteen. Still, ECT has saved the lives of some patients whose depression was so severe that they were suicidal or at risk of harming others.

Other Forms of Therapy

Exercise is one of the easiest treatments for depression. It gets the heart pumping and the neurotransmitters moving. "Runner's high" is a common term for the happier mood many people feel after vigorous aerobic exercise.

Phototherapy (treatment with special lights) can help people with seasonal affective disorder. The lights help to maintain even moods during the winter months, when days are short.

Support groups and self-help groups also help people with depression. Members of the group exchange information about the disorder and about current research on treatment and medication. Support group members help each other develop ways to live with the symptoms of depression and cope with the need for continuous therapy or medication. Support groups can also help family members adjust to living with a person experiencing depression.

Acupuncture is a treatment that uses special needles inserted at specific locations in the skin. It is based on principles of Chinese medicine that link health and illness to energy flow throughout the body. Acupuncturists use needles to rebalance energy flow that has become unbalanced. The effects of acupuncture may be similar to the runner's high of aerobic exercise.

Four

Suicide and Depression

The musical group Nirvana came to an end in 1994, when its founder, the talented singer-songwriter Kurt Cobain (1967–1994), killed himself. According to Kurt's cousin, Bev Cobain, many members of the Cobain family have been affected by "the demons of depression, drug addiction, and suicide." A psychiatric nurse, Bev Cobain believes that Kurt Cobain had untreated bipolar disorder (manic depression) at the time of his suicide.

In her book about teen depression, Bev Cobain wrote a letter to her late cousin, Kurt. Part of the letter is about Courtney Love, Kurt Cobain's wife, and

how a suicide affects the family members who survive. Part of the letter is about hope: "If you had been appropriately treated for depression," she wrote, "instead of trying to medicate yourself with drugs and alcohol, the outcome could have been different. Nobody has to die because of depression or drug addiction."
—Bev Cobain, R.N.C., *When Nothing Matters Anymore: A Survival Guide for Depressed Teens.* Minneapolis, MN: Free Spirit Publishing, 1998, p. 8.

There are many effective treatments that can help people with depression and bipolar disorder. However, in the most serious cases of depression, people often believe that suicide is the only way out.

Warning Signs

Some of the warning signs that a friend or family member is considering suicide are similar to the signs of depression:

- Problems with sleep, appetite, energy, and pain that does not go away
- Loss of interest in friends, family, activities, and pleasures
- Feeling sad, empty, discouraged, hopeless, and worthless

There are other signs that can indicate that depression has become so severe that suicide is a possibility:

- A sudden crisis at school or at home
- A serious change in behavior
- Using street drugs and alcohol
- Taking drug overdoses
- Running away from home
- Acting recklessly and violently
- Acquiring guns or weapons
- Cutting oneself
- Talking about dying; for example, "You won't miss me when I'm dead"
- Preparing for dying; for example, making a will or giving away one's favorite CDs
- Having a close friend or family member commit suicide
- Having made a prior attempt at suicide

If friends or family observe some or all of these signs, they should contact an adult, a doctor, a counselor, a coach, or a suicide hot line for immediate assistance. Conversation about suicide—especially from someone who has tried suicide in the past—is a genuine 911 emergency.

Who Commits Suicide?

The U.S. National Center for Health Statistics keeps track of information about illnesses and deaths in the United States, and the American Association of Suicidology (AAS) analyzes, or interprets, the data every year. Statistics show that suicide is the third leading cause of death for people between the ages of ten and twenty-four, and that boys commit suicide more often than girls. More children and teens die from suicide than from cancer, heart disease, AIDS, birth defects, stroke, pneumonia, influenza, and lung disease combined, with only accidents and homicides causing more teen deaths. Children and teens age fourteen and younger commit suicide much less often (307 suicides in 2000) than those in the fifteen to twenty-four age group (3,994 suicides in 2000). Elders over age sixty-five are at highest risk (5,306 suicides in 2000). Untreated depression is believed to be the leading cause of suicide in this age group. For more information, visit the AAS Web site, www.suicidology.org.

Getting Help

People who are thinking about suicide often talk to their friends about it first. They may ask their friends to promise secrecy, and friends may fear they are betraying a trust if they ask an adult for help.

This creates a situation that calls for a true life-and-death decision. Helping a friend get treatment for suicidal feelings—even when that friend is so upset that he or she does not want treatment—can lead to an opportunity for apologies, forgiveness, and future friendship. Not getting treatment may lead to suicide—and an end to friendship, happiness, and life.

Here are steps friends can take to help when there is talk of suicide:

- Encourage your friend to tell a parent, doctor, school counselor, coach, or member of the clergy.
- Encourage your friend to call a suicide hot line.
- Ask an adult for help yourself. Choosing to get help instead of remaining silent may make the difference between life and death for your friend. Trust your instincts.
- If there is an immediate danger of suicide, call 911. The 911 operators know how to get help in an emergency.

Five

Living with Depression

Treatment, therapy, support groups, and medication are the main roads to wellness for anyone who has depression or bipolar disorder. Treatment requires time and patience, however, and there are some adjustments that have to be made in everyday living.

Adjustments at School

Special-education placements can help students continue their education while they are undergoing treatment for depression. Parents, teachers, principals, and special educators can work together to create an individualized education plan (IEP) for students who need one. An IEP may include a late start to the school day, one-on-one work with a teacher's aide, regular sessions with a school psychologist, and tutoring during school absences and hospitalizations. With an IEP, students with depression or bipolar disorder can maintain their academic progress throughout treatment so they can graduate on time with their friends.

Keeping Up at School During Treatment

The Child and Adolescent Bipolar Foundation (www.bpkids.org) offers many strategies that can help students with depression to keep up at school:

- *One-on-one or shared special-education aide in class*
- *Two sets of textbooks for home and school*
- *Reduced homework or extended deadlines when energy is low*
- *Late start to the school day in cases of morning fatigue*
- *Recorded books if there are problems concentrating while reading*
- *Calculator if there are problems concentrating on math problems*
- *Unlimited access to drinking water and a bathroom*
- *Identifying a "safe place" to go when feeling overwhelmed*
- *Having regular sessions with a school psychologist or social worker*
- *Summer day camp or summer school to help stay current*

Adjustments at Home

If you have depression, the most important thing you can do to help yourself feel better is to continue with your treatment plan. If a parent, brother, sister, or friend is suffering from depression, the following strategies can help you and everyone else adjust to the illness.

- Remember that the person with depression still loves you even if he or she cannot show it.
- Remember that you are not to blame for depression. Depression is a medical condition that requires treatment.
- Understand that the person with depression may be ashamed of the illness and its symptoms. Unpleasant feelings are a big part of depression.
- Understand that the person with depression may be worrying about you, especially if he or she is a parent who is unable to spend as much time with you as before.
- Ask if you can go to a therapy session.
- Ask the therapist to answer your questions about depression.
- Ask for regular family meetings to discuss the depression, the treatment, and how family members can create a plan to help during times of severe illness.

- Stay focused on living your own life.
- Reach out to friends, grandparents, and community members who can support you and your family during treatment for depression.

Managing Feelings of Anger, Disappointment, and Frustration

If you are the person with depression, then you already know that dark moods and feelings are part of your illness. If a parent, brother, sister, or friend is the one with depression, then you may be surprised by how angry, disappointed, and frustrated you are about someone else's illness.

Anger, disappointment, and frustration are all natural emotions, especially when a serious illness occurs. It is natural to want people with depression to feel better right away so that life can get back to "normal." We don't want them to have dark thoughts, we don't want them to sleep all day every day, we don't want them drinking too much or using drugs, and we certainly don't want them to harm themselves.

Understanding and accepting our own negative emotions requires the same strength, patience, and support that people with depression need to stick to their treatment plans. Treatment for depression takes a long time.

Learning Optimism

"Learned helplessness" and "learned optimism" are terms linked to the work of psychologist Martin Seligman. Seligman observed that people with depression often endure their illness passively, without even trying to get treatment. This is especially true for people whose depression may be a reaction to abuse or injury.

People with learned helplessness act as if they have been taught to believe they can never escape from the dark feelings of their depression. But if they have learned to react to their illness with helplessness and hopelessness, they can also learn optimism, which is the best medicine in the world for hopelessness.

An optimist believes that treatment for depression can lighten the heavy feelings of sadness, helplessness, hopelessness, and discouragement about life. An optimist believes that treatment can help people manage and cope with the darkest moods of depression. An optimist believes that treatment for depression can help all of us find our way back to a life filled with friendship, love, creativity, and joy.

Glossary

anesthesia: a medical procedure that uses a special medication, called an anesthetic, to block pain in specific parts of the body or to put someone to sleep during surgery or electroconvulsive therapy

antidepressant: prescription medication that may be used along with psychotherapy to treat depression

bipolar disorder: formerly called manic-depression, this disorder causes cycles of major depression that alternate with extreme energy highs

chronic: a disorder that continues for a very long period of time clinical trial: experiment that uses volunteer patients to test the safety and effectiveness of a new treatment before it is approved for general use

cyclothymia: bipolar mood cycles that occur at frequent intervals

diagnosis: the process of performing medical exams and laboratory tests to identify specific illnesses so doctors can determine the correct treatment

dopamine: a neurotransmitter that researchers have linked to depression

dysthymia: milder than major depression, dysthymia causes feelings of sadness and emptiness that may continue for years

electroconvulsive therapy (ECT): often called shock therapy, ECT uses electrical impulses to cause a controlled seizure that can help the body's neurotransmitter system work more effectively; like surgery, ECT requires hospitalization and anesthesia

genetics: the study of DNA, chromosomes, genes, and inheritance patterns; many cases of depression are linked to genetic causes and tend to run in families, passing from parent to child in the same manner as skin color, eye color, and size hormones: chemicals produced by the body's endocrine (glandular) system to carry messages to all the organs of the body, transferring information and instructions from the brain to the organs about body processes like growth, sleep, and digestion

major depression: also called unipolar depression, this is a serious disorder that can interfere with daily life; if left untreated, it can last for months or years

melatonin: a hormone that helps the body regulate its cycles of wakefulness and sleep

neuron: a nerve cell; one end of the neuron receives chemical messages and the other end transmits them

neuroreceptor: a location at the receiving end of a neuron that recognizes a specific neurotransmitter or medication and allows it to attach to the neuron

neurotransmitter: a chemical produced by the body's nervous system to carry messages from neuron to neuron, transferring information and instructions from the brain to the body about thoughts, emotions, and behaviors norepinephrine: a neurotransmitter that researchers have linked to depression

over-the-counter medication: medication that people can buy in drugstores without a doctor's written instructions

phototherapy: treatment for seasonal affective disorder that uses special lights

placebo: a process or a substance without medical properties; researchers sometimes use sugar pills or water injections as placebos in clinical trials that test new medications

postpartum depression: depression that sometimes occurs in new mothers after (post) childbirth (partum); sometimes called the "baby blues," postpartum depression is linked to hormonal changes

prescription: a recipe for medication written by a doctor; prescription medications can be used only with a doctor's supervision

psychiatrist: a medical doctor who specializes in treating people who have mental disorders that affect the mind and the body psychologist: a researcher who studies behavior or a counselor who specializes in treating people whose mental disorders affect their behavior and social interactions

psychopharmacologist: a researcher who studies psychiatric medications and how they affect thoughts, feelings, and behaviors

psychotherapist: a mental health counselor, social worker, psychologist, or doctor who helps individuals or groups of people in talk therapy

psychotherapy: often called talk therapy, psychotherapy helps people understand their own thoughts, feelings, behaviors, and relationships with others

recurrence: the return of illness after a period of improvement and better health

remission: a period of time when health improves and signs of illness are reduced

Saint-John's-wort *(Hypericum perforatum)*: an herbal supplement that may act as an antidepressant screening: testing or examining people who are healthy to see if they have an increased risk for specific disorders; screening can help with the early diagnosis and treatment of serious disorders like depression

seasonal affective disorder (SAD): a form of depression linked to receiving too little sunny daylight, SAD sometimes affects people at the start of the winter season

selective serotonin reuptake inhibitor (SSRI): a type of antidepressant medication that helps the body use serotonin more effectively

serotonin: a neurotransmitter that researchers have linked to depression

suicide: killing oneself

symptoms: signals of illness that people feel inside themselves; during medical exams, doctors will ask people to describe their symptoms

synapse: the space between two neurons

Further Resources

Books

Cobain, Bev. *When Nothing Matters Anymore: A Survival Guide for Depressed Teens.* Minneapolis: Free Spirit, 1998.

Desetta, Al, and Sybil Wolin, editors. *The Struggle to Be Strong: True Stories by Teens About Overcoming Tough Times.* Minneapolis: Free Spirit, 2000.

Garland, E. Jane. *Depression Is the Pits, But I'm Getting Better: A Guide for Adolescents.* Washington, DC: Magination Press, 1997.

Irwin, Cait. *Conquering the Beast Within: How I Fought Depression and Won . . . and How You Can Too.* New York: Times Books, 1999.

Nelson, Richard E., and Judith C. Galas. *The Power to Prevent Suicide: A Guide for Teens Helping Teens.* Minneapolis: Free Spirit, 1994.

Pamphlets and Fact Sheets

KidsHealth.org. *Going to a Psychologist, Psychiatrist, or Therapist.* www.kidshealth.org

U.S. National Institute of Mental Health. *What to Do When a Friend Is Depressed.* NIH Publication 01-3824, 2001. www.nimh.nih.gov

Online Sites and Organizations

American Academy of Child and Adolescent Psychiatry
3615 Wisconsin Avenue NW
Washington, DC 20016
www.aacap.org

American Association of Suicidology
4201 Connecticut Avenue NW, Suite 408
Washington, DC 20008
www.suicidology.org

American Psychiatric Association
1000 Wilson Boulevard, Suite 1825
Arlington, VA 22209
www.psych.org

American Psychological Association
750 First Street NE
Washington, DC 20002
www.apa.org

National Alliance for the Mentally Ill
Colonial Place Three
2107 Wilson Boulevard, Suite 300
Arlington, VA 22201
www.nami.org

Depression and Bipolar Support Alliance (DBSA)
730 N. Franklin Street, Suite 501
Chicago, IL 60610
www.dbsalliance.org

National Mental Health Association
2001 N. Beauregard Street, 12th floor
Alexandria, VA 22311
www.nmha.org

U.S. Centers for Disease Control and Prevention (CDC)
1600 Clifton Road, NE
Atlanta, GA 30333
www.cdc.gov

National Human Genome Research Institute (NHGRI)
Building 31, Room 4B09
31 Center Drive, MSC 2152
9000 Rockville Pike
Bethesda, MD 20892
www.genome.gov

U.S. National Institute of Mental Health (NIMH)
6001 Executive Boulevard
Room 8148, MSC 9663
Bethesda, MD 20892-9663
www.nimh.nih.gov

Index

Pages in *italics* indicate illustrations

About the Author

Faye Zucker is a writer and editor who likes to work on books about medicine, psychology, and education. She attended Public School 110 and Hunter College High School in New York City. She has a B.A. in linguistics and an M.A. in librarianship from the University of Chicago. Currently, Faye is happily working for Sage Publications in Thousand Oaks, California, as executive editor of Corwin Press, Inc. She is a firm believer in mental health treatment, which in her case included individual psychotherapy, group psychotherapy, and medication. Treatment works!

I thank the following friends and colleagues for their comments and for reading and improving the manuscript of this book:

Joan E. Huebl, Paula Edelsack, Kristine Lundquist, Diane Tropper, and Martha Langer. Thanks, too, to my editors, Meredith DeSousa and Nikki Bruno, at Scholastic Library Publishing.